CW00503213

JOHN MERRILL'S

WHITE   PEAK

CHALLENGE WALK

ABOUT JOHN N. MERRILL

John combines the characteristics and strength of a mountain climber with the stamina and athletic capabilities of a marathon runner. In this respect he is unique and has to his credit a whole string of remarkable long walks. He is without question the world's leading marathon walker.

Over the last fifteen years he has walked more than 100,000 miles and successfully completed ten walks of at least 1,000 miles or more.

His six major walks in Great Britain are -
Hebridean Journey .... 1,003 miles
Northern Isles Journey .... 913 miles
Irish Island Journey... 1,578 miles
Parkland Journey... 2,043 miles
Lands End to John o'Groats... 1,608 miles
and in 1978 he became the first person (permanent Guinness Book of Records entry) to walk the entire coastline of Britain — 6,824 miles in ten months.

In Europe he has walked across Austria — 712 miles — hiked the Tour of Mont Blanc, completed High Level Routes in the Dolomites, and the GR20 route across Corsica in training! In 1982 he walked across Europe — 2,806 miles in 107 days — crossing seven countries, the Swiss and French Alps and the complete Pyrennean chain — the hardest and longest mountain walk in Europe, with more than 600,000 feet of ascent!

In America he used the the world's longest footpath — The Appalachian Trail — 2,200 miles — as a training walk. He has walked from Mexico to Canada via the Pacific Crest Trail in record time — 118 days for 2,700 miles. In Canada he has walked the Rideau Trail.

During the summer of 1984, John set off from Virginia Beach on the Atlantic coast, and walked 4,226 miles without a rest day, across the width of America to Santa Cruz and San Francisco on the Pacific Ocean. His walk is unquestionably his greatest achievement, being, in modern history, the longest, hardest crossing of the USA in the shortest time — under six months (178 days). The direct distance is 2,800 miles.

Between major walks John is out training in his own area — the Peak District National Park. As well as walking in other parts of Britain and Europe he has been trekking in the Himalayas five times. He has created more than ten challenge walks which have been used to raise more than £250,000 for charity. From his own walks he raised over £80,000. He is author of more than ninety books, most of which he publishes himself. His book sales are in excess of 2 million.

JOHN MERRILL'S

WHITE PEAK CHALLENGE WALK

by

JOHN N. MERRILL

Maps and Photographs

by John N. Merrill.

a J.N.M. PUBLICATION

1988

a J.N.M. PUBLICATION

JNM PUBLICATIONS,
WINSTER,
MATLOCK,
DERBYSHIRE.
DE4 2DQ

This book is copyright under the Berne Convention. All rights are reserved. Apart from any fair dealing for the purposes of private study, research, criticism or review, as permitted under the Copyright Act, 1956, no part of this publication may be reproduced, stored in a retrieval system, or transmitted in any other form by any means, electronic, electrical, chemical, mechanical, optical, photocopying, recording or otherwise, without the prior permission of the copyright owner. Enquiries should be addressed to the publishers.

Conceived, edited, typeset, designed, marketed and distributed by John N. Merrill.

© Text and route — John N. Merrill 1988

© Maps and photographs — John N. Merrill 1988

First Published — 1983; reprinted 1984, 1985 and 1986 as John Merrill's Peak District Challenge Walk — ISBN 0 907496 43 1.
This edition — September 1988

ISBN 0 907496 77 6

Meticulous research has been undertaken to ensure that this publication is highly accurate at the time of going to press. The publishers, however, cannot be held responsible for alterations, errors or omissions, but they would welcome notification of such for future editions.

Printed by The Amadeus Press Ltd, Huddersfield

Set in Futura — medium and bold.

Companion volume — John Merrill's Dark Peak Challenge Walk.

CONTENTS

VIEW FROM CALLING LOW — LATHKILL DALE IN CENTRE — CALES DALE ON LEFT

INTRODUCTION

The fine traditional market town of Bakewell is the central point of the Peak District, and a logical starting point for a challenge walk in the area. My aim has been to create—

1. a circular walk, using footpaths as much as possible.
2. a walk that could be accomplished within a day—10 hours.
3. a challenge, making the route as rugged as possible, but one that is within everyone's capability.
4. to combine as much scenic variety in the route as possible.

Bearing these points in mind, the walk takes you through limestone scenery—plateaux and dales; across gritstone moorland and past rocky outcrops; and along river valleys. The paths are in the main little used ones. Several of the well-known areas such as Monsal Dale will be seen from different angles providing stunning views. En route are numerous historical sites and ancient monuments. You pass through several villages where there are shops and inns to 'help you' on your way.

I first walked the route over three mornings just before Christmas in appalling conditions—wind, cold and rain. As I walked I checked the route, making careful notes. I have since walked it seven times—usually in eight hours—and can assure you that it is a splendid circuit!

By the end of 1985 more than 3,500 people have completed the walk in an average time of 10 hours. The longest on record is 16 hours, and the fastest—running—is 4 hrs 14 minutes; this was their third attempt! Many have used the walk to raise money for charity, and so far approximately £55,000 has been raised.

All that remains for me to say is—have a good walk, let me know how you get on, and may the sun shine all day and may your feet remain dry and blister free!

Happy walking!

John N. Merrill

JOHN N. MERRILL Derbyshire. 1986

P.S. Since the 1986 edition a further 2,000 people have walked the route and the total raised for charity is in excess of £75,000. With the publication of my Dark Peak Challenge, and as this book was ready for reprinting I have changed the title from Peak Challenge to the White Peak Challenge. This is to clarify the two walks.

HOW TO DO IT

The whole route is covered by the Ordnance Survey maps — 1:25,000 Outdoor Leisure Map — The White Peak 1:50,000 Sheet No. 119 — Buxton, Matlock and Dovedale

The walk is devised to be done in a single day, allowing between 8-10 hours. There is no criterion to walk it in a day — it is not a competition — and if you want to spend a weekend over it, that's fine. There are hostels, bed and breakfasts, hotels and campsites on or very close to the route to allow you to do this. For those who complete it a four colour embroidered badge and completion certificate is available from JNM Publications.

The route has been carefully mapped with walking notes, and you should have no difficulty walking round. However, during the course of time stiles change, gates change colour and signs disappear. At the time of publication the maps and notes are correct.

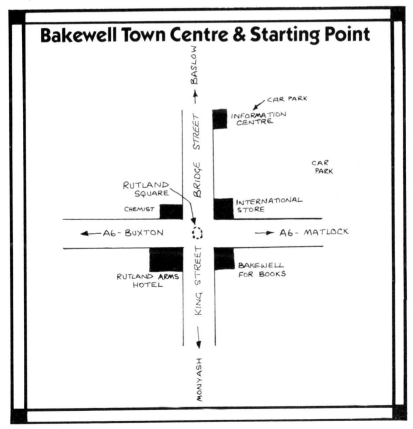

Bakewell Town Centre & Starting Point

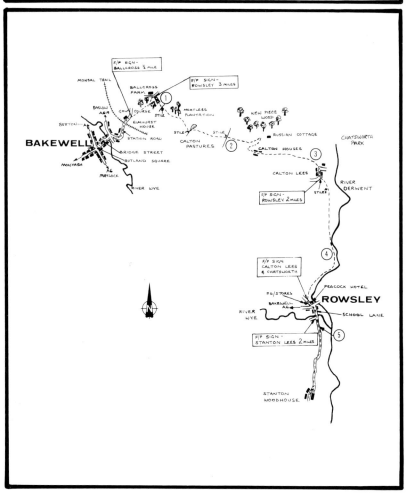

MONSAL TRAIL—One of three disused railway lines in the National Park, now transformed into pedestrian ways. This one, opened in 1981, stretches for 8 miles, from Bakewell to Chee Dale, and was formerly the line from Matlock to Buxton.

BALLCROSS—Former packhorse way to Sheffield and Chesterfield through the steep wood. In 1678 it was paved at a cost of £3.19.8d. (£3.98p). The stone was later removed to build the present road, in 1810. The cross and base have long since been lost.

RUSSIAN COTTAGE—Built like a log cabin, with intricately carved window frames and gable ends. Originally built for a visit by a Russian Czar, it is now a gamekeeper's cottage.

BAKEWELL TO ROWSLEY—5 Miles

River Wye to River Derwent

WALKING INSTRUCTIONS

From Rutland Square walk out of Bakewell along Bridge Street, past the Information Office and across the Wye Bridge. Bear right and ascend Station Road. At the entrance to the small factory complex, turn right up the minor road towards the Golf Course and cross the 'Monsal Trail'. Opposite Elmhurst House, as footpath signposted, turn right and ascend the wide track through the golf course and woodland to Ballcross.

Turn right at the top as signposted and follow the walled track towards Rowsley. Continue along a grass track to a stile on the immediate right of a large pond. Go through a gate beyond and cross the open pastures of Calton Pastures to join a track on the immediate left of a plantation. At the track junction near Russian Cottage, turn sharp right and descend the track, first to Calton Houses and on to Calton Lees, a mile away.

On gaining the road turn right, and, where the road bears right 300 yards later, turn left, as footpath signed, and follow the path to Rowsley, 2 miles away. Cross the first field to a wooden stile on your left, before descending to the valley floor and the River Derwent. Follow the well-stiled path along the valley to Rowsley, entering the outskirts after passing underneath a railway arch. Turn left along the road to the Peacock Hotel, A6 and the centre of Rowsley.

BAKEWELL

A fine old market town on the banks of the River Wye, crossed by a 14th Century five-arched bridge—one of the oldest in the country. The town is the administrative centre of the National Park, and the Market Hall is an Information Centre. There are many old buildings rich in history and legend.

Avenel Court—on King Street; dates from mediaeval times and is close to the old Town Hall and Courtroom built in 1602 by Sir John Manners.

Parish Church—dedicated to All Saints; dates from Norman times. The Vernon Chapel includes the tombs of Dorothy Vernon and Sir John Manners who, in the 16th Century, eloped from nearby Haddon Hall—one of the most romantic legends of the Peak District.

The Rutland Arms—where Jane Austen stayed, and which is featured in her novel 'Pride and Prejudice'. It was the cook at the Rutland Arms who, in about 1859, misunderstood her instructions and made the now famous Bakewell Puddings. They are still made to the original recipe.

RUTLAND ARMS HOTEL, BAKEWELL

RIVER WYE—BAKEWELL

PEACOCK HOTEL, ROWSLEY

Rowsley to Robin Hood's Stride—4 Miles

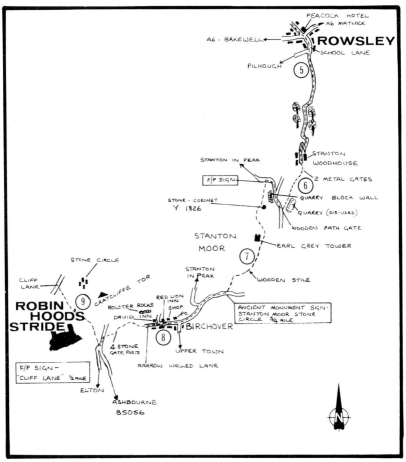

Thornhills of Stanton in Peak in 1832 to commemorate the passing of the first Reform Bill. The stone with the coronet, large Y and date 1826 commemorates the renowned Duke of York.

BIRCHOVER—Gritstone village famed for its quarries, whose stone has been used in many notable buildings. Close to the Druid Inn is Rowter Rocks, where rooms, passageways, stairs and armchairs have been carved. At first believed to have been the work of the Druids, but now known to be the eccentric work of a member of the Eyre family. Several of the stones are rockable.

Just down the lane from the inn is a small 18th Century chapel built by Thomas Eyre in 1717. In the porch is a plaque to Joan Waste who, believed to be a heretic, was burnt to death in the Windmill Pit, Derby, on August 1st 1556.

ROWSLEY TO ROBIN HOOD'S STRIDE
—4 Miles

River Valley to gritstone outcrops.

WALKING INSTRUCTIONS

Cross the A6 road and walk along School Lane. Just after crossing the River Wye, turn left along the farm road; signposted to Stanton Lees, 2 miles. ¾ mile later, at the drive entrance to Stanton Woodhouse, turn sharp right and follow the twisting farm road around the house and past the farm. Pass through two metal gates and continue ascending on a grass track lined with gorse. Just beyond a large wooden gate the track forks; keep to the left, passing a deep fenced quarry on your left. Gain the minor road via a small wooden gate. Turn right, and at the road junction beyond turn left, signposted for Stanton in Peak.

300 yards up here turn left, as footpath signposted, and follow the path onto Stanton Moor. Ascend the first field on a faint path to the plantation wall, where there is a small stone stile. Enter the wood and gain a well-defined path. In time this merges into the main path on the moor. Continue ahead to the Earl Grey Tower. ¼ mile later, at a wooden stile, bear right and follow the wide path down to the road. Turn right and walk along the level road before descending into Birchover village. Keep the Druid Inn on your right as you descend a narrow lane past the chapel and back into the fields. Where the farm track turns sharp left, keep straight ahead on the path to a stile. Just past a ruined barn, descend to the road. Bear left along it before turning right at the road junction and following the signposted path to Robin Hood's Stride.

PEACOCK HOTEL, ROWSLEY—Built in the 17th Century, the porch lintel bears the date 1652, and a peacock is on top of the turret above. The peacock is the crest of the Manners family—the Dukes of Rutland, owners of nearby Haddon Hall. The inn was originally built as a private residence by John Stevenson, 'man of affairs' to Grace, Lady Manners. The school bearing her name, in Bakewell, was founded by her in 1636.

STANTON WOODHOUSE—Former early 17th Century shooting lodge of the Dukes of Rutland, now a private house. When the Duke of Rutland was restoring his ancestral home—Haddon Hall—early this century, he used the house as his base.

STANTON MOOR—Exceptional viewpoint over the Derwent Valley and Matlock. The heather and bilberry gritstone moorland has several ancient monuments, including a Bronze Age stone circle known as the Nine Ladies; and over seventy burial mounds of the beaker folk have been identified. Finds from excavations can be seen in Weston Park Museum, Sheffield. The Earl Grey Tower on the eastern side was built by the

DOORWAY LINTEL—PEACOCK HOTEL, ROWSLEY

RED LION INN—BIRCHOVER

JOHN MERRILL AT ROBIN HOOD'S STRIDE

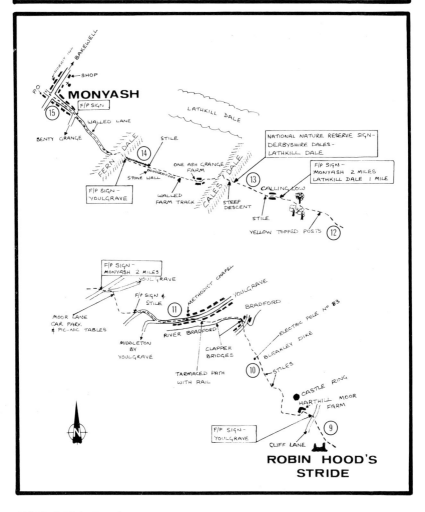

YOULGREAVE—Limestone village dominated by the 15th Century perpendicular tower of the Parish Church. Inside is a unique font incorporating a holy water stoup; a 12th Century monument to Sir John Rossington who holds a heart; and an alabaster panel to Robert Gilbert and family. The church was one of the few to have an 'official dog whipper'. In 1716 he was paid 7p annually to whip the dogs out of the church before divine service. Derbyshire's unique well-dressing ceremony takes place here in June.

ONE ASH GRANGE—Formerly associated with Roche Abbey near Maltby in South Yorkshire. To here misbehaven monks were sent for punishment. A barn has been converted to a camping barn.

11

ROBIN HOOD'S STRIDE TO MONYASH
—6 Miles
Gritstone outcrops to limestone plateau

WALKING INSTRUCTIONS

Ascend the track towards Robin Hood's Stride, keeping straight ahead where the track turns right to the cottage beneath Cratcliffe Tor. Keep the Stride on your left as you reach the top and cross the fields, using the stiles to 'Cliff Land'. Walk towards Harthill Moor Farm before bearing left around the building and descending to the footpath junction at the bottom of the field. Turn right, and a field later turn left along an ascending track before beginning the descent to the River Bradford. The path is defined in places and well-stiled to Bleakley Dike and on to Bradford.

Turn right at the road, and almost immediately left, along a walled path to the clapper bridge. Cross and turn left, and walk beside the River Bradford to the next clapper bridge. Don't cross it, but keep to the right-hand side of the river and begin ascending the tarmaced railed and stepped path to Youlgreave. At the road, almost opposite the Methodist Church, turn left and follow the road, keeping right at the Middleton junction. Just round the next corner on your right is the path sign and stile. Ascend the field to the next stile before curving right to Moor Lane car park and picnic tables. Turn left at the road, and at the junction 100 yards away cross the road and follow the well-stiled and marked path with yellow-topped posts across the fields to the wood and Calling Low Farm. Walk through the farm yard and descend the fields to Cales Dale, reached by a steep final descent.

Cross the dale floor and ascend to One Ash Grange, passing the farm on its righthand side. Continue along the farm track and, where it curves right, keep straight ahead with the limestone wall on your left. In due course ascend a stile on your left and descend to the shallow Fern Dale. On the other side join a walled track which you follow to Monyash. At the road—Rakes Road—keep straight ahead to the village green and cross.

ROBIN HOOD'S STRIDE—Two gritstone towers whose distance apart—22 yards—is said to be the length of Robin Hood's stride. The rocks provide pleasant scrambling, and are often called 'Mock Beggars' Hall', for the pinnacles look like chamineys. Opposite is Cratcliffe Tor, a popular rock climbing outcrop. At its base is a hermit's cave with a crucifix carved in the 14th Century. On the 'moor' beyond the rocks is a Bronze Age stone circle with four upright stones—the tallest in the Peak District. Castle Ring is the remains of an Iron Age fort.

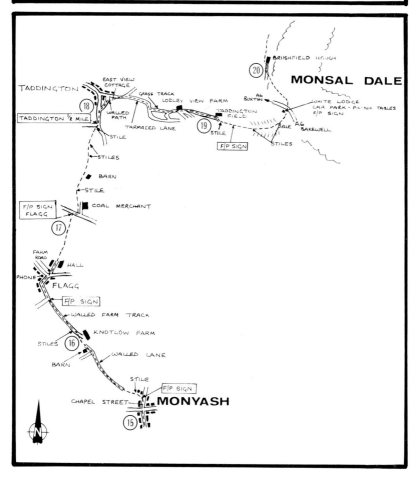

FLAGG—situated on the limestone plateau 1,000 ft. above sea level. Annual Point to Point races organised by the High Peak Hunt are held here at Easter. The 16th Century Hall is renowned for its ghosts, and has a skull which, if moved, causes unexplained happenings to occur. The name Flagg means a place where turf was dug for fires.

TADDINGTON—Limestone village whose 18th Century charm has been saved by the bypass. The church is largely 14th Century, with a magnificent 16th Century brass to the Blackwell family and their eleven children. The 18th Century Hall is one of the very attractive smaller impressive buildings of Derbyshire. Like Flagg Hall, ghost stories still linger. At one time a farmer owned the Hall, and every Monday rode to Bakewell Market. He always returned drunk, and one night he walked into the house without opening the door. He is said to still haunt the building.

13

MONYASH TO MONSAL DALE—5 Miles
across the limestone plateau

WALKING INSTRUCTIONS

From the green, walk along Chapel Street for 75 yards and turn left at the car park; follow the footpath-signed path across the fields to the lefthand side of the row of houses, skirting round the last one to a stile. The path to Flagg is very well-stiled, first to a walled track which you follow to just past a barn on your left. Cross further fields, keeping Knotlow Farm on your right. Beyond, gain the farm track and follow this to the road, which you walk along into Flagg. Cross the main road and walk up the farm road with the Hall on your immediate right. Keep straight ahead through the farmyard to the gate and track. Keep on this and cross the field beyond to the stile and Flagg path sign. Turn right, and left almost immediately, and ascend the stile; walk in the field immediately on the left of a coal merchant's. The path beyond is faint, but all the stiles are there as you pass close to a barn on your right before ascending slightly and curving to the road junction and Taddington road sign.

Descend the road and take the first walled track on your right. As you near the houses, turn right and follow the walled grass track around the buildings before descending to the eastern edge of Taddington village at East View Cottage. Turn right along the No Through Road. ¼ mile along here turn left along a walled grass track and gain the lane to Lodley View Farm. Keep to the left track here and descend to Taddington Field Farm. Turn right and left almost immediately, and descend the shallow dale before curving left to White Lodge car park, picnic tables and A6 road ½ mile away.

MONYASH—Former lead mining centre of the High Peak with its own Barmote Court for settling local mining disputes. The market cross on the green dates back to 1340, and an annual market is still held there in August. The church dates from the 12th Century.

HOBBIT INN—MONYASH

CRATCLIFFE TOR

MARKET CROSS—MONYASH

HOLME BRIDGE, BAKEWELL

BAKEWELL—VICTORIA MILL WHEEL

Monsal Dale to Bakewell—5 Miles

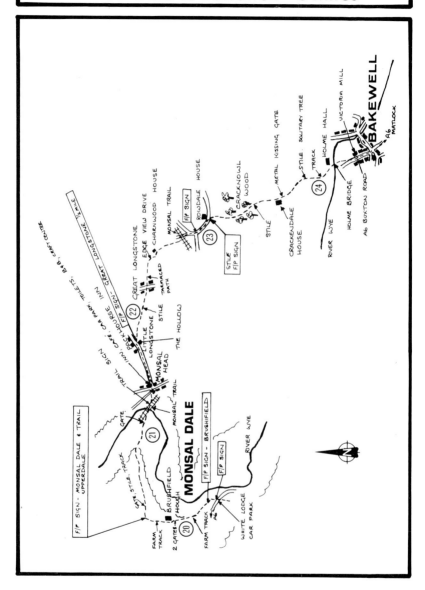

HOLME BRIDGE—Built in 1664 for use by pack-horse teams—hence the low parapet. Upstream is Lumford Mill, a former 18th Century spinning mill where 300 people worked.

VICTORIA MILL—Late 18th Century corn mill in use until 1945. The water wheel has been removed and is adjacent to the building; it measures 16 ft. in diameter by 13 ft. 6 ins. wide.

MONSAL DALE TO BAKEWELL—5 Miles
Hilly route back to Bakewell

WALKING INSTRUCTIONS

Cross the A6 road and follow the path across a small stream before turning left and ascending the path to Brushfield. In the early part there are numerous steps to ascend. Gain the farm road via a stile. At the entrance to the farm turn left, as signposted, and walk round the lefthand side of the buildings to the farm track. Follow this to the path-signed junction. Here turn right — 'Monsal Dale, Trail and Upperdale'. The path is a walled track for much of its length. As you descend, keep to the righthand track and gain the railway viaduct — the Monsal Trail. Cross the viaduct and ascend to your left to Monsal Head.

Descend the road to Little Longstone. Just past the Packhorse Inn, turn right and, as signposted, cross the fields to Great Longstone. Keep straight ahead along a tarmaced path to the recreation ground. Cross this to Edge View Drive. Walk along this road to its end, and on the right of Charnwood House is the path across the fields to the railway bridge and road junction. Pass under the bridge and turn left along the road to Rowdale House. Turn right on the path, and after the first field ascend through Cracknowl Wood to the fields and Crackendale House. Keep the house on your right to gain a metal kissing gate. Ascend the gentle field beyond. Just over the brow is the stile and the descent to Bakewell. Descend the track to Holme Hall on your immediate left. Cross Holme Bridge and turn left along the A6 road — Buxton Road — back to Rutland Square.

MONSAL HEAD—Perhaps the finest viewpoint in Derbyshire. Down to the perfect curvature of Monsal Dale, with its 120 feet high railway viaduct, now part of the Monsal Trail. The view up the Wye Valley to Cressbrook is particularly attractive. On the river are coots, moorhens, mallard ducks and occasional kingfishers. The dale is rich in flora — monkey flower, butter and the early spring flowers of lesser celandines, cowslips and wood anemones.

GREAT LONGSTONE—Attractive limestone village with small green and cross. Longstone Hall, a classical styled red-brick building, dates from 1747. The church is partly 13th Century, with an exceptionally well-preserved 15th Century nave roof with moulded beams.

HOLME HALL—Beautiful Tudor building with mullioned windows; built in 1626.

AMENITIES GUIDE

Village /Town	B&B	YHA Hostel	Camp-site	Inn	Rest-aurant	Shop	P.O.	Transport (Bus)
BAKEWELL	*	*		*	*	*	*	*
ROWSLEY	*			*	*	*	*	*
BIRCHOVER	*		*	*	*	*	*	*
ELTON (¾ mile off route)		*	*	*	*	*		
YOULGREAVE	*	*		*	*	*	*	*
MONYASH	*		*	*		*	*	*
FLAGG				*				*
TADDINGTON				*		*	*	*
MONSAL HEAD	*			*	*	*		*
LITTLE LONGSTONE				*				*
GREAT LONGSTONE	*			*		*	*	*

INNS

ROWSLEY	GROUSE AND CLARET INN
BIRCHOVER	DRUID INN
	RED LION INN
MONYASH	HOBBIT INN
FLAGG	PLOUGH INN
TADDINGTON	QUEEN'S ARMS INN
MONSAL HEAD	MONSAL HEAD HOTEL
LITTLE LONGSTONE	PACKHORSE INN

Y.H.A.

BAKEWELL — FLY HILL—Tel. Bakewell (062981)2313

YOULGREAVE — FOUNTAIN SQUARE
Tel. Youlgreave (062986) 518

BED AND BREAKFAST

BAKEWELL	Milford House Hotel, Mill Street, Bakewell, DE4 1DA. Telephone: Bakewell 2130
	Mrs. K.H.Pheasey, Bourne House, The Park, Bakewell. Telephone: Bakewell 3274
ROWSLEY	Peacock Hotel, Rowsley Telephone: Darley Dale 3518
BIRCHOVER	Mrs. C. Hobbs, Brickfields Cottage, Eagle Tor, Birchover. Telephone: Winster 459
	Mrs C.V. Kelsey, Rocking Stone Farm, Birchover, Derbyshire. Telephone: Winster 356
YOULGREAVE	M. Shimwell, Church Farm, Youlgreave, DE4 1US. Telephone: Youlgreave 305
	The Bulls Head Hotel, Youlgreave, Bakewell, Derbyshire. Telephone: Youlgreave 307
MONYASH	Lea Hurst, Monyash. Telephone: Bakewell 2575
	The Hobbit Inn, Monyash, Bakewell. Telephone: Bakewell 2372
MONSAL HEAD	Castle Cliffe Private Hotel, DE4 1NL Telephone: Great Longstone 258
	Merlin House, Ashford Lane, DE4 1NL. Telephone: Great Longstone 475
	Monsal Head Hotel Telephone: Great Longstone 250
GREAT LONGSTONE	Mrs. R. McGoverne, Willow Croft, Station Road, Great Longstone. Telephone: Great Longstone 576
CAMPING BARN	A converted barn to a hut type accommodation, with bed space and cooking facilities. Only one on the route at—One Ash Grange, above Cales Dales. Details and bookings to— Peak National Park Study Centre, Losehill Hall, Castleton, Derbyshire, S30 2WB.

20

LOG

DATE...................... TIME STARTED...................... TIME COMPLETED......................

| Route Point | Mile No | Time | | Comments/ |
		Arr.	Dep.	Weather
Bakewell—Rutland Square	0			
Ballcross	1			
Calton Pastures	1½			
Calton Houses	2¼			
Calton Lees	3¼			
Rowsley—A6	4¾			
Stanton Woodhouse Farm	5¾			
Stanton Moor—Tower	6¾			
Birchover—Red Lion	8			
Robin Hood's Stride	9			
Harthill Moor Farm	9¼			
River Bradford	10¼			
Moor Lane Car Park	11¾			
Calling Low	12¾			
One Ash Grange Farm	13½			
Fern Dale	14¼			
Monyash—Cross	15			
Flagg	16½			
High Well—Taddington	18			
Taddington Field	19			
A6 Road	19½			
Brushfield Hough	20			
River Wye	21			
Monsal Head	21½			
Little Longstone	22			
Great Longstone	22½			
Rowdale House	23			
Crackendale House	23¾			
Holme Hall	24¼			
Bakewell—Rutland Square	25			

TRAIL PROFILE—3,600 ft. of ascent

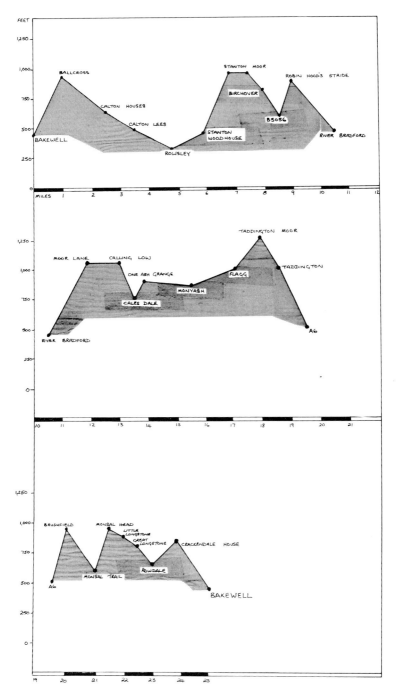

OTHER BOOKS BY JOHN N. MERRILL PUBLISHED BY JNM PUBLICATIONS

DAY WALK GUIDES —

SHORT CIRCULAR WALKS IN THE PEAK DISTRICT
LONG CIRCULAR WALKS IN THE PEAK DISTRICT
CIRCULAR WALKS IN WESTERN PEAKLAND
SHORT CIRCULAR WALKS IN THE STAFFORDSHIRE MOORLANDS
SHORT CIRCULAR WALKS AROUND THE TOWNS AND VILLAGES OF THE PEAK DISTRICT
SHORT CIRCULAR WALKS AROUND MATLOCK
SHORT CIRCULAR WALKS IN THE DUKERIES
SHORT CIRCULAR WALKS IN SOUTH YORKSHIRE
SHORT CIRCULAR WALKS AROUND DERBY
SHORT CIRCULAR WALKS AROUND BAKEWELL
SHORT CIRCULAR WALKS AROUND BUXTON
SHORT CIRCULAR WALKS AROUND NOTTINGHAMSHIRE
SHORT CIRCULAR WALKS ON THE NORTHERN MOORS
40 SHORT CIRCULAR PEAK DISTRICT WALKS
SHORT CIRCULAR WALKS IN THE HOPE VALLEY

INSTRUCTION & RECORD —

HIKE TO BE FIT...STROLLING WITH JOHN
THE JOHN MERRILL WALK RECORD BOOK

CANAL WALK GUIDES —

VOL ONE — DERBYSHIRE AND NOTTINGHAMSHIRE
VOL TWO — CHESHIRE AND STAFFORDSHIRE
VOL THREE — STAFFORDSHIRE
VOL FOUR — THE CHESHIRE RING
VOL FIVE — LINCOLNSHIRE & NOTTINGHAMSHIRE
VOL SIX — SOUTH YORKSHIRE
VOL SEVEN — THE TRENT & MERSEY CANAL

DAY CHALLENGE WALKS —

JOHN MERRILL'S WHITE PEAK CHALLENGE WALK
JOHN MERRILL'S YORKSHIRE DALES CHALLENGE WALK
JOHN MERRILL'S NORTH YORKSHIRE MOORS CHALLENGE WALK
PEAK DISTRICT END TO END WALKS
THE LITTLE JOHN CHALLENGE WALK
JOHN MERRILL'S LAKELAND CHALLENGE WALK
JOHN MERRILL'S STAFFORDSHIRE MOORLAND CHALLENGE WALK

MULTIPLE DAY WALKS —

THE RIVERS' WAY
PEAK DISTRICT HIGH LEVEL ROUTE
PEAK DISTRICT MARATHONS
THE LIMEY WAY
THE PEAKLAND WAY

COAST WALKS —

ISLE OF WIGHT COAST WALK
PEMBROKESHIRE COAST PATH
THE CLEVELAND WAY

HISTORICAL GUIDES —

DERBYSHIRE INNS
HALLS AND CASTLES OF THE PEAK DISTRICT & DERBYSHIRE
TOURING THE PEAK DISTRICT AND DERBYSHIRE BY CAR
DERBYSHIRE FOLKLORE
LOST INDUSTRIES OF DERBYSHIRE
PUNISHMENT IN DERBYSHIRE
CUSTOMS OF THE PEAK DISTRICT AND DERBYSHIRE
WINSTER — A VISITOR'S GUIDE
ARKWRIGHT OF CROMFORD
TALES FROM THE MINES by GEOFFREY CARR
PEAK DISTRICT PLACE NAMES by MARTIN SPRAY

JOHN'S MARATHON WALKS —

TURN RIGHT AT LAND'S END
WITH MUSTARD ON MY BACK
TURN RIGHT AT DEATH VALLEY
EMERALD COAST WALK

COLOUR GUIDES —

THE PEAK DISTRICT ....Something to remember her by.

SKETCH BOOKS — by John Creber

NORTH STAFFORDSHIRE SKETCHBOOK

EQUIPMENT NOTES—some personal thoughts

BOOTS—preferably with a leather upper, of medium weight, with a vibram sole. I always add a foam cushioned insole to help cushion the base of my feet.

SOCKS—I generally wear two thick pairs as this helps to minimise blisters. The inner pair of loop stitch variety and approximately 80% wool. The outer a thick rib pair of approximately 80% wool.

WATERPROOFS—for general walking I wear a T shirt or shirt with a cotton wind jacket on top. You generate heat as you walk and I prefer to layer my clothes to avoid getting too hot. Depending on the season will dictate how many layers you wear. In soft rain I just use my wind jacket for I know it quickly dries out. In heavy downpours I slip on a neoprene lined cagoule, and although hot and clammy it does keep me reasonably dry. Only in extreme conditions will I don overtrousers, much preferring to get wet and feel comfortable.

FOOD—as I walk I carry bars of chocolate, for they provide instant energy and are light to carry. In winter a flask of hot coffee is welcome. I never carry water and find no hardship from doing so, but this is a personal matter.From experience I find the more I drink the more I want. You should always carry some extra food such as Kendal Mint Cake for emergencies.

RUCKSACK—for day walking I use a climbing rucksac of about 40 litre capacity and although excess space it does mean that the sac is well padded and with a shoulder strap. Inside apart from the basics for the day I carry gloves, balaclava, spare pullover and a pair of socks.

MAP & COMPASS—when I am walking I always have the relevant map—usually 1:25,000 scale—open in my hand. This enables me to constantly check that I am walking the right way. In case of bad weather I carry a Silva type compass, which once mastered gives you complete confidence in thick cloud or mist.

PEAK CHALLENGE

Badges are white cloth with figure embroidered in four colours and measure —
3" wide x 3½" high.

BADGE ORDER FORM

Date completed ....

Time ....

NAME ....

ADDRESS ....

....

Price: £2.00 each including postage, VAT and signed completion certificate.

From: J.N.M. Publications, Winster, Matlock, Derbyshire, DE4 2DQ
Tel: Winster (062988) 454 — 24hr answering service.

********* **You may photocopy this form if needed** ********

THE JOHN MERRILL WALK BADGE — walk this route twice or complete
another John Merrill's challenge walk and send details and cheque/PO for £2.00
for a special circular walk badge. Price includes postage and VAT.

REMEMBER AND OBSERVE
THE COUNTRY CODE

ENJOY THE COUNTRYSIDE AND RESPECT ITS LIFE AND WORK.

GUARD AGAINST ALL RISK OF FIRE.

FASTEN ALL GATES.

KEEP YOUR DOGS UNDER CLOSE CONTROL.

KEEP TO PUBLIC PATHS ACROSS FARMLAND.

USE GATES AND STILES TO CROSS FENCES, HEDGES AND WALLS.

LEAVE LIVESTOCK, CROPS AND MACHINERY ALONE.

TAKE YOUR LITTER HOME—PACK IT IN, PACK IT OUT.

HELP TO KEEP ALL WATER CLEAN.

PROTECT WILDLIFE, PLANTS AND TREES.

TAKE SPECIAL CARE ON COUNTRY ROADS.

MAKE NO UNNECESSARY NOISE.

ABOUT THE WALK —

Whilst every care is taken detailing and describing the walk in this book, it should be borne in mind that the countryside changes by the seasons and the work of man. I have described the walk to the best of my ability, detailing what I have found on the walk in the way of stiles and signs. Obviously with the passage of time stiles become broken or replaced by a ladder stile or even a small gate. Signs too have a habit of being broken or pushed over. All the route follows rights of way and only on rare occasions will you have to overcome obstacles in its path, such as a barbed wire fence or electric fence.

The seasons bring occasional problems whilst out walking which should also be borne in mind. In the height of summer paths become overgrown and you will have to fight your way through in a few places. In low lying areas the fields are often full of crops, and although the pathline goes straight across it may be more practical to walk round the field edge to get to the next stile or gate. In summer the ground is generally dry but in autumn and winter, especially because of our climate, the surface can be decidedly wet and slippery; sometimes even glutonous mud!

These comments are part of countryside walking which help to make your walk more interesting or briefly frustrating. Standing in a farmyard up to your ankles in mud might not be funny at the time but upon reflection was one of the highlights of the walk!